SLAYING
YOUR
FEARS

REMOVING THE MONSTERS
THAT THREATEN YOUR HAPPINESS

SLAYING
YOUR
FEARS

VOLUME I

DA-NEL EUWINGS

To my future Self - you're welcome
To my Son - you're the Legacy
To my Paladin - you're my Rock

TABLE OF CONTENTS

Foreword 1

The Monster – Complacency 6

The Monster – Misplaced Loyalties 31

The Monster – Indecisiveness....................................53

The Monster – Guilt...74

Epilogue 94

About the Author..97

FOREWORD

ONE THING FOR SURE IS YOU DESERVE SOME CREDIT.
You are holding this book because you are aware of a deafening fact that is too loud to ignore anymore. The fact is, your fears have their nasty, greedy hands on the steering wheel of your life, and they are steering your life in a direction that you have begun to question. Subconsciously, you have been questioning your life's direction for some time. (Later in this book we'll discuss how your dreams have likely been dominated by your fears.) Yes, your fears have been driving and they are the absolute worst drivers ever. How?

They thrive on haste and impulsivity, so they have no regard for your safety or the safety of others as they zigzag and bump you all over the place. They disregard the impact of their choices when they do not use their turn signal, or any indication of change in their path that directly affects others. They have no regard for your happiness as you zoom past opportunities for possible growth and prosperity. They stink and because you are a captive passenger you begin to smell like them and reek of a negative and unhealthy aura. They do not have good sense of direction because their internal compass of good judgement and sense has been weakened by groupthink autopilot mentality. They do not consult maps, do not have a plan, and instead guess their way along the road, refusing to ask for help. They do not take care of their health, they are not alert, and they put you in danger by falling asleep at the wheel, leaving you confused about where you are and what to do next. They do not pay attention at all. Instead of facing forward and focusing primarily on what is ahead – your future - your fears choose to dart side to side, focusing an unsafe amount of time on external distractions. They become hypnotized, almost paralyzed, by the rearview mirror as if they are trapped in the things from behind - trapped in the past.

Clearly, your fears are the worst kind of driver to be steering your life. Your fears are deafening, deceptive and convince you that they are protecting you, shielding you, guiding you away from risks, dreams, changes, goals and needs that could enrich, even save, your life. This driver has talked for you and talked over you because you have remained silent and unsure of yourself and unsure of your intended destination. This driver has done the thinking because you have remained comfortably in autopilot. This driver does not care about lacking a clear destination because anywhere will do.

"If you don't know where you are going, any road will do."

— *Lewis Carroll*

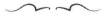

Perhaps you have recently needed to address a health issue. Perhaps you have recently needed to apologize to someone you hurt. Perhaps your fears have given you an off-putting odor, making you difficult and sometimes offensive to be around. Perhaps you have adopted traits such being prickly, bitter, fickle, offensive, jealous, cynical, dishonest, or what some would call having a negative aura that reeks and repels. Perhaps you have recently been reminded of how precious life is. Perhaps you have realized that your fears have driven you past the same mile-marker year after year and you have not made any forward progress, but you have instead allowed your fears to drive you around in time-wasting circles. Perhaps you have noticed the same cars around you on this road who have also been part of this mindless circling. Perhaps you have recently taken inventory of your life, your accomplishments, your losses, your hopes, your missteps, your talents. Perhaps you have recently come to realize that your fears have driven you along a path that has led to waste, regret, injury, embarrassment, and futility. You have been yelling at this driver, but you have given them power too long, so they do not hear you…yet. Now what? Perhaps you've found yourself being driven by a new driver, but you eventually realize this driver does not have your best interests either. Although they have taken you onto a different road, it is a road that continues to waste your most valuable resources – time, energy, money.

Did you notice the damaging and derailing effects of allowing such drivers to steer your life? Did you notice how your fears, just like the monsters they are, behave like possessive bullies and infect your thinking? Did you notice that you are merely along for their ride, lacking confidence in your ability to making sound decisions, lacking clarity of direction, lacking an endearing reputation, an aura that is attractive, that you are lacking the benefit of being alongside successful and progressive people?

There are different types of fears. In this book you will explore a few fears that have grown into your monster. You need to identify them and explore the reasons they exist for you, how you are feeding them and how to slay them – how to expose these fears for what they really are and honestly accept their impact in your life and on your future prospects.

"Slay them?!" Is that what you just said to yourself? Breathe. I get it. Perhaps you have felt it was simpler and easier to find ways to cover up, excuse, justify, ignore, or pray away your monsters. There is a big difference between resigning to escapism and acceptance and facing your monsters head on. There is a big difference between covering up the odors and mess your monsters have created and rolling up your sleeves to clean house. Let's face it; After a while, there is not much that quick fixes like air freshener or a fancy rug can do to cover up your monster as it grows and even multiplies.

I get it though. Discussing your fears can be a scary and daunting thing. Fear isn't something to be avoided. Use fear to your advantage.

Fear is a wonderful opportunity to learn about yourself. Face your fears is a risk and taking risks are a natural part of life so you can truly immerse yourself in the real act, and process, of living. This means making time, like you've begun to do, by acknowledging your fears and this allows you to sort through them and identify them. In this way your fears are no longer the unknown or faceless monsters, and they may not be quite as big and seemingly undefeatable.

Your fears are attacking your money, body, spirit, and mind and are keeping you from truly thriving. Therefore, you have found yourself living in survival mode. Your fears have you in a continual fight or flight mode which is reactive and is dangerous. You know that you deserve to prosper, shine, and grow. You know that you want healthier relationships, amazing adventures, and fulfilling experiences. You know that you are tired of the embarrassment, emptiness, or exhaustion your fears have caused You know that your monsters do not deserve to dominate and wreck further havoc on your life, your peace, or your health. You know these monsters need to be slayed – and I'm here to help you.

Shall we begin?

CHAPTER 1

THE MONSTER—COMPLACENCY

"The tragedy of life is often not in our failure, but rather in our complacency; not in our doing too much, but rather in our doing too little; not in our living above our ability, but rather in our living below our capacities."

— *Benjamin E. Mays*

WHY SLAY THIS FEAR

ONE OF MY FAVORITE THINGS IS MY HUGE ELECTRIC fleece throw blanket. Not only because is it weighted, which gives me the feeling of being wrapped in a safe snug cocoon, but I also keep it scented with lavender or magnolia essential oil. Once my blanket is warmed it smells absolutely wonderful and makes me feel even more relaxed – and relaxed I was. This blanket was what I'll call my couch potato partner in crime. Whenever I wanted to veg out and binge watch TV shows, this partner helped to keep me in the perfect position and stupor while I mentally slow-cooked all my cares away. I used to fall asleep on my couch many nights only to awaken to terrible neck, back and hip pain. For a time, I would go days without sleeping in my own bed because I would prefer my couch and my warm and comfortable couch potato partner.

It was almost as if it was a type of security blanket. Imagine, a forty-plus-year-old woman with her very own stylish and sweet-smelling warm security blanket. Whenever I wanted to protect myself from the cold struggles and disappointments of 'adulting' I would take steps to lock myself into my own type of time machine. In my time

7

machine, my cocoon, I was able to shut down and shut out noise that was trying to make me see and hear things that was too annoying or uncomfortable to face at times. When I did get up from under it, I was reminded of how cold things were without it. Although I felt better after emerging to finally eat, shower, or groom myself, my couch potato partner was there waiting to swaddle me back into my cocoon of comfort and stillness. In this comfort zone of my creation, I put up my barriers and defenses. I did not want anyone or anything to disturb my groove, my vibe, my pace, my space. I found a way to do the minimum in some areas of my life. Whenever more was required, I found a real or imagined reason to insist on doing what felt safe, comfortable, and familiar. Interestingly, I became aware that some of my acquaintances had similar partners in crime, after all, like-minded people often recognize each other, don't they?

By no means was I a lazy person or a stranger to hard work. I was an accomplished and talented woman. I was accustomed to doing backbreaking work for many years as a single mother – even requiring major surgery for a work-related injury. There were times however, where I felt pushed and pulled farther and farther away from my couch potato partner. At times I imagined what real free would be like, a change of my comfortable norm. At times I imagined how all my creative senses could be stimulated by getting out from under sleepy warmth and into the cold. I imagined how it could feel to stretch out into another position rather than the same limited fetal position that my couch potato partner had me warmly and tightly cocooned in.

Remember, this book does not offer medical advice in any form yet there is something to be said about the importance of having a healthy selfcare routine - to curtail burnout -including counselling, exercise, and diet. Notice the key word - healthy. There was little health benefit my couch potato partner offered me other than serving the purpose of keeping me weighed down with little interest to get up, do better and become better. Perhaps I was experiencing periodic blues and slumps. That's very normal for anyone, but my couch potato partner was the wrong kind of partner in this state. This partner wasn't just snuggling me but was actually squeezing me into a near mummy-like state; I was functioning but not having real depth, breadth, or lasting purpose in my actions.

There is a big difference between succumbing to habitual mental lethargy and escapism, and making time to relax, unwind, pause, regroup, and enjoy the comforts of being in your own home – not to mention the cost savings, which will be discussed in another chapter.

This is where I confess to you that I came to realize it wasn't about my electric fleece blanket. It was about what it represented for me. It represented a state of mind that was at the root of actions or inactions that did not enrich my life in the long run. It represented denial, guilt, and resentment that I preferred to cover up rather than face and rectify. It represented a stagnant, slow moving, slow growing place where I dared anyone to disturb, move, or change me. It represented an acceptance and preference for predictability, routine and sameness – on my terms. It represented a mindset that became comfortable and easy to me. It represented a monster called complacency.

What is complacency? One dictionary defines it this way: "A feeling of smug or uncritical satisfaction with oneself or one's achievements. A self-satisfaction especially when accompanied by unawareness of actual dangers or deficiencies. A feeling of quiet pleasure of security, often while unaware of some potential danger, defect, etc."

Complacency is not a lack of intelligence, nor a lack of access to resources, nor a lack of talents. This is a monster that smothers and hoards your best assets, preventing you from using them to maximum potential and also acquiring new ones. In fact, in an interesting twist, this monster convinced me that these things could be better utilized by other people. How? I was content in my comfort zone so I was all too happy to 'help' others take what I had begun and run with it or letting others 'pick my brain' so they could accomplish their goals, do the stretching, experimenting, and growing that I was content to not doing. I told myself I was a good person in allowing other people to shine, while I 'fell back'. I did not see the urgency or necessity. As long as my comfort zone operated on my terms my monster kept me feeling safe, content, and functional. There seemed to be a predictable and stable comfort in risking little by doing little. This is the monster complacency. This is also what I refer to as life lethargy - being grateful to be alive but not really living. This is also the origin of dangerous traits such as envy, competition, comparison, and waste of precious resources. How so? When you are truly gifted and know there is something special about you, there are times that it seemed your gifts, your light needed to shine and put to better use. It was as if you would burst if you didn't get up, stretch, and grow and this made you feel resentful, stifled, and stuck.

If you're honest about this monster, you'll realize the path it is bullying you toward – spending time watching others live and thrive while you either spend time and money competing or comparing, or worse, you aren't motivated to explore and regularly act on your own unique purpose and talents with focus, consistency, and strides toward improvement.

This monster personifies what it means to be a Hating Blocker – getting in between someone and their path. Let's look at the various ways this monster operates. Remember how this monster kept me in a tight fetal position? It blocked my ability to stretch and my desire to stop the physical and mental pains I felt day after day. Remember how this monster smelled so good – like lavender oil? It kept me listening only to its sweet voice, tickling my ears with what I wanted to hear and blocking what I needed to hear such as sound advice, valid counselling or pointed criticism. Anything that didn't smell or sound as sweet was rejected or resisted at best. Remember how this monster kept me swaddled many nights on my couch instead of being in my own bed? It limited my movements, blocking me from exploring other areas of my home that could have sparked different interests, actions, and creativity. Remember how this monster was only on my couch? Instead of having a set allotted time for chilling and binging, it blocked me from setting healthy parameters for how long and for what purpose. This monster, rooted in the fear of discomfort, fear change, and loss of security began to grow when I started to take a few things for granted, particularly my most precious resource - time. Allow me to elaborate.

"You may delay, but time will not."

— *Benjamin Franklin*

One of the things that exists in a complacent state of mind is lack of awareness of just how fleeting real time is. In my comfort zone I stubbornly and possessively dictated how my time would be used. In a complacent stupor, you create a kind of time machine where you ignore deadlines, postpone professional or personal development activities, or stroll and surf on your past accolades and accomplishments, for instance. Your reasoning is that you can create another time to start and finish, that there was always tomorrow or next year, however, your time machine remains stuck in your comfortable here-and-now, rarely advancing forward in real time. Time is one of our most precious resources and a complacent state mind does not appreciate that reality until it is too late. Sometimes, the loss of a family member or a beloved celebrity are occasions that may temporarily shock us back into real time awareness and jumpstart a dormant desire. Sadly, this monster gets refueled by your habits and successfully convinces you there is always a justified excuse and always a way around what you consider to be uncomfortable. (This monster has some ugly relatives like procrastination, doubt and guilt which will be discussed in later chapters.) Also, complacency does not mean that a person functions at a snail's pace. In fact, their speed of operation is usually to rush and hurry through the undesirable tasks that could no longer be postponed, delegated, or ignored. Their aim to resume their preferred routine in their comfort zone. In fact, this is what they consider an accomplishment – a stubborn refusal to submit to things that disrupts their established order – and is something they may even boast about like a banner of pride.

Another false sense of security this monster creates is an overconfidence and even an overestimation of your talents, attributes, and skills. In a complacent way of existing, this monster is a devilish sycophant, a deceptive flatterer who likes to tickle and play with your ego. It has to be said that your ego can have a useful part of your personality as it is closely related to confidence and self-esteem, however as we'll cover in this book, your monsters come into existence when aspects of your personality aren't regularly assessed for their honest impact and effect on your decision making, and your time habitually left unmanaged. This is why ego is instead more related to pride and arrogance when left unchecked and becomes a monster that causes regret and disruption and needs to be slayed. Your ego reminds you of how your past has served you; favors you have extended to people, your awards and promotions, flattery from social media fans, or even your romantic conquests. Your ego gives false reassurance that you have a bottomless Life bank account that doesn't need replenishing, no deposits needed. While clogging your ears with its warm honied words, your ego does not listen to valid advice and even shakes it off, perhaps even accusing the messenger of being a hater. This monster is fueled by the past and wants you to keep feeding it by remaining in the past rather than making necessary progress and improvement in your life in order to move forward. This monster thrives off fruitless and repetitive actions because after all, isn't that the definition of insanity – doing the same things the same way over and over but expecting a different result? Therefore, complacency can be tricky to identify and even harder to battle with – but it is not an impossible task and this fear can be slayed.

I came up with an acronym for ego and it means Exaggerated Grandiose and Oblivious. This acronym has come in useful whenever I needed to look myself square in the eyes and check myself. Here's why. When you are in survival mode you are often in a fight or flight mode as well. In this hurried and anxious state, sometimes reality is exaggerated, and facts are blurred and unclear. In fight mode, I was incredibly reactive, busily doing damage control, being abuzz with activity, defending my past honor – a literal busy bee. In flight mode, I was hiding, existing as a shell, stubbornly doing nothing substantive, or in a resentful autopilot mode doing what has always worked, pacifying myself or others.

A grandiose person is not necessarily the loudest or flashiest person and this trait isn't solely related to fashion or style but instead can be evident in other ways. When in fight mode, especially when I lacked understanding of the type of monster I was dealing with, I was either overextending myself or overcompensating for areas I wasn't ready to admit I needed to improve – and boy, was my monster watching all of this! So, my promises got bigger, my deadlines got lengthier and my progress delayed far longer than necessary – a clear waste of my resources, and sometimes others'.

When evaluating your health, a health professional will usually first check your temperature to verify any need for further evaluation or tests, and if it was at an extreme level then corrective action was recommended. Right? Similarly, while in a complacent state, your temperature can be said to be lukewarm – mostly comfortable but not extreme enough to propel you into concern, alarm, or action prompting positive change for yourself. Only when we experience an extreme temperature of discomfort do we take steps to adjust.

Being hot makes people want to remove layers such as clothing, people or things that crowd, weigh down, stifle, suffocate or take up space. Being cold makes people want to add buffers, tighten their circles, and protect what is exposed to harsh elements. Both of these extreme temperatures cause discomfort, disorientation, and disconnection from your preferred safe cocoon – it means acting and making change.

Your monster doesn't want you to feel the extremes and it seduces you to just be cool, to coast, to ride the comfortable, predictable, safe tides you're drifting on, nestled in that warm blanket cocoon. It doesn't care if you lose out because you are set in your preferred ways, your system, your preferences.

There was a time I was confronted with personal and professional changes that I didn't anticipate and wasn't ready to face; however, in order to 'adapt' the discomforts forced upon, like a rude awakening snatching a blanket off me, I was making clever and quick decisions to survive. I eventually learned they weren't good for my long-term happiness. If you've similarly experienced the energy-draining and talent-stunting hypnotic effect of this fear, and you watched opportunities pass you by, I invite you to read on to learn strategies that can slay this monster.

GET READY TO SLAY

OK SO, HOW DO YOU EVEN BEGIN TO DEAL with a complacent mindset? First, your goals, your standards and your methods self-care need to be reevaluated because this monster will capitalize on what you don't know – or what you won't face – about yourself. Let's look at how to get unstuck, how to stay creative, qualifying your goals, and being self-disciplined.

Do you feel like your life has been in a rut? Why is it that our lives rarely change, even when we're miserable?

You lack the knowledge necessary to make a change. You might know that you need to be more confident, but you might also lack the knowledge of how to develop confidence. Not all skills are available at our fingertips. You might need to do a little studying before a change is possible.

You don't know specifically what you want. For example, if you think you might like to be a fireman, but also think becoming an accountant sounds interesting, as well as enrolling in medical school, you're likely unfocused and have become stuck which is different than having multiple talents and interests. At some point, it's necessary to make a clear decision and set a goal. This of it like this; If you can't choose a vacation destination, you're stuck at home. Staycations are nice and sometimes safety and cost effective however in order to expand your horizons, clearer focus and targeted goals with timelines can save you time and protect your peace as well.

You lack willpower or fail to use it effectively. Willpower is limited, but it's great for creating new habits and behavioral patterns. Sticking with a task after the urge to quit surfaces can develop willpower. Continue for another 5 minutes. Increase the amount of time each week until you can work through the urge to give up. Use your willpower to develop small habits that can grow into useful routines.

You can't deal with being uncomfortable – and this was an especially troubling area for me since I frequently preferred comfortable sameness and predictable control. Anxiety, nervousness, and fear are great for preventing you from jumping off a 10-story building. But they're worse than worthless when it comes to keeping you stuck. Some level of discomfort accompanies any change, but your emotions are misleading you. Reassure yourself that you're not in any real danger. Use your logic to talk yourself through it. Use the logical part of your brain to override your primitive instincts to run from this monster and instead face it and transform this fear.

If this is a true struggle, there are many techniques to lower your levels of discomfort to more manageable levels. Meditation, prayer, and counseling are a few that can be beneficial. Start small and push through slight discomfort. Your ability to handle the bigger and scarier situations will grow with experience.

Be honest with yourself and make sure you don't give up too quickly. Change can take time because most of the change you ultimately see won't reveal itself until at least a large portion of the work has been completed. Your early efforts show little results, but things are happening behind the scenes. It's necessary to persevere to see a meaningful change in your life.

Learn to be a finisher. Start completing all the little tasks in your life. Using a small example for instance; If you decide to walk on the treadmill for 20 minutes, keep going until you're done. Avoid letting yourself off the hook until an activity is 100% complete.

Making any change can be a challenge. Understanding your roadblocks to change can enhance your ability to bring about meaningful changes in your life. Have an objective and develop habits that support that objective. Learn to lower and deal with uncomfortable emotions. You have everything within in you necessary to create a spectacular life. Go for it!

But what if your complacency because you've lost your creative mojo? I can definitely empathize. As the world scene continues to change and sometimes turn things upside down, it seems we have to pivot and be pushed into directions that we weren't ready to delve into yet, but I've learned that harnessing your ingenuity will make your life more meaningful and enjoyable. Creativity is so important and welcome more innovation and inspiration into your daily activities versus stuck in joyless complacency, which will stop fueling this monster you're battling.

Learn to experience more joy. Creativity flourishes when you think positively. Find your passions and cultivate them. Embrace challenges with curiosity. Observe the conditions that help you get "in the zone." Improve your physical health. This is a straightforward necessary way to relieve stress and boost our immune system. Those who think resourcefully also cope better with aging and experience fewer declines in their cognitive functions.

Don't forget to strengthen your relationships. A sense of imagination can even enhance your personal relationships. Break out of the same old conflicts by searching for common ground (this was discussed in the Chapter Misplaced Loyalties). Look at challenging situations from the other person's perspective and try out a different response.

Remember that while it's comfortable being surrounded by and thrilled by our own genius and ideas, collaboration is integral to the creative process. Include others in your mountainous or new projects. Tap into the experts that you've vetted or hired or work alongside. Help create a more cooperative atmosphere where colleagues complement each other's strengths rather than competing.

Enjoy the pleasure of developing your own gifts. With persistence and an open mind, you'll expand your skills for responding to all kinds of challenges. Brainstorm. Generating ideas is usually the first step in the creative process. Put aside any judgments and just let the options flow – an opportunity to push the proverbial envelope and being more experimental.

Before you're overwhelmed with all your great ideas; however, take time to pause, listen and incubate. Before inspiration hits, there's usually a quiet time while we digest our ideas. Help your unconscious mind along by taking a quiet walk or a relaxing shower. Routine tasks like purging junk from your home, kneading bread, painting, rearranging furniture or clearing a cupboard for instance, have been amazingly inspirational and can trigger insights.

Then, begin to act by planning for how to implement your ideas. Regard every attempt as a learning experience even if the immediate results fail to pan out. Remember that successful people succeed because they take more risks.

It's at this point I have to include something that helps me – remembering to laugh and to lighten up. This doesn't mean that you have to be a giggler 24/7 especially if you're more reserved. But I've come to see how keeping balance and allowing for levity can totally free up your fertile mind. Humor is an immensely powerful tool for lowering inhibitions and seeing things more vividly – after all, this monster isn't expecting you to find any glimmers of hope let alone much reason to laugh. That's why it needs to be slayed!

Change your routine. Any adjustment to your usual way of doing things can help you take a fresh look at life. Take an alternate route to work or visit a coffee shop on the other side of town. Expand your horizons by looking for ways to experience novelty on a regular basis.

Observing the details is also crucial because complacent habits and monotonous rote can cause you to overlook outdated information or routines that no longer work for you or your projects and tasks. On the other hand, you can re-invent the most familiar aspects of your life by viewing them from a fresh angle.

If you're struggling with this, think of getting a hobby. Make the most of your leisure time with creative outlets that incorporate your passions and seek inspiration. Surround yourself with whatever you find invigorating. Visit art museums or go camping or tapping into your inner child and spend more time playing with your kids (or nieces, cousins, grandchildren, etc.) and getting caught up in their excitement each time they see something new. Transform your life into a work of art by tapping into your creative side. Once you discover and develop your passions, you'll be on your way to feeling more accomplished and fulfilled.

Remember to do what makes you genuinely happy. You may already have an idea about what you might like to do creatively, but you may be afraid of failure, so you don't try at all. However, the only failure is if you give up before you start. So, what if you fall flat on your face? So, what if people are judging you? Adopt the "you only live once" attitude and go for it!

Yes, failures will happen – success isn't possible without the failed attempts that you learned from (this will be discussed in the Chapter Pessimism) and if anyone preaches instant success to you without failed attempts, they are lying to you. So, try again. Let's say that you feel your true calling is film making. You take a class, but your teacher doesn't like your work. What do you do? Do you give up or keep going? The answer's obvious: pick yourself up and keep learning the craft! Take another class or create a film on your own. As long as you're enjoying yourself, learning, and practicing, you'll create your own version of success!

Don't stop thinking and get overly comfortable. Of course, you never really stop thinking. However, you need to always be thinking new thoughts, solutions, and ideas, especially in mundane situations. You mustn't just accept that things are done a certain way - you need to expand your thinking and keep coming up with new ways to do old tricks. So, stay inspired! When you follow what truly inspires you, creativity just comes along for the ride. Let's say you always wanted to start a business. That doesn't sound terribly creative on its own, especially if it's a type of business that already exists. But your inspiration will spark your creativity as you decide how your business will stand out from the competitors.

Having the discipline to stay true to your values, needs, mission however, is what will keep you from being distracted or discouraged by your competitors. Your self-discipline is a huge factor in the amount of success you achieve. Accomplishing big goals often requires doing things we don't enjoy. Discipline is basically the ability to get yourself to do things you don't really feel like doing.

Everyone lacks the necessary discipline at times. We can't always get ourselves to do the things that we know we should be doing. Then we feel bad about it. Then we beat ourselves up and feel even worse. Don't let this happen to you! Usually, you won't feel so bad if you can generally get a handle on your discipline.

Additional arsenal to keep this monster at bay or some of the following strategies I've employed to bring self-discipline back under control:

Take it easy on yourself. Feeling bad with excessive self-berating or negative self-haranguing makes most people less capable, not more capable. Everyone slips at times; just recognize that this is one of those times for you. Move on and move forward. Staying with that emotion accomplishes nothing.

Focus on your motivation for the goal. Why is this goal relevant to you? Imagine how it will feel to accomplish it. Motivation is just about the only way to get yourself to do something you don't want to do. Ideally, you could find a way to make the activity easy and enjoyable.

Making your goals challenging but as realistic and manageable as possible. The smaller the barrier, the more likely you are to perform the activity. For example, if you want to exercise daily, make it super easy at first. Start with just 5 minutes. It's easy to get started with 5 minutes. Next week you can add 5 more. Also, find a form of exercise that's convenient (and safer) for you. You're likely to find that if you can just get over the barrier of getting started, then you'll go ahead and complete the whole task. So, make getting started easier for you.

Try to make it enjoyable. Exercise might be far more enjoyable if you join a cultural dance class, a basketball league, or a walking group for instance, instead of running on a treadmill by yourself. Working on the computer might be a lot easier out on your deck with the birds and the trees in the background. In other words, think about a way to perform the activity as enjoyably as possible.

Have long term goals but don't overwhelm yourself and recoil into bad habits that kept you comfortable - stay in the present. We're great at making ourselves feel bad about things that either happened in the past or haven't happened yet. Avoid thinking about the unpleasant activity until it's time. If you sit around and spend an hour dreading something, it makes it a lot harder to actually do it. Staying in the present is part of the reason why Buddhist monks are so calm; they spend all day trying to only focus on their current activity. Then they move on to the next thing and repeat. Their goal is to do everything with the same attention and calmness. Using this technique can go a long way toward helping you with discipline.

Don't let that monster get in your head telling you to quit! Stick with it. You might exercise for a week straight and then fall off the wagon. Start all over again with the first step. You're not a robot; you can't realistically expect to be perfect 100% of the time. Set a goal for continuous improvement rather than perfection.

A certain amount of discipline is required to do anything worthwhile unless you're lucky enough to genuinely enjoy all the steps involved. When you get stuck, take it easy on yourself and go back to your source of motivation. Then make the activity as easy and enjoyable as possible. Rinse and repeat.

Regardless of the nature of your goal – fitness, financial, spiritual, professional, etc. - the more control you have over yourself, the more successful you can become.

Finally, remember your objective is to acknowledge and address self-sabotaging habits that threaten your happiness and fuel those awaiting monsters you're battling. Self-sabotage could be defined as deciding you want something and then making sure it doesn't happen. Have you ever found yourself close to achieving a goal, only to throw it all away at the last moment? Did you look back later and kick yourself for being so foolish? I definitely have as most of us have and there are several possible explanations, ranging from a need to control the situation to feeling unworthy. But regardless of the cause, the solutions are similar. I challenge you to work to eliminate self-sabotage from your life by considering a few strategies I've employed over the years.

In order to get out of the unfulfilling robot- mode of comfort and complacency, regularly observe yourself. Look back at the times you've sabotaged yourself or come up short. You probably try to justify the sabotaging behavior in your mind but, ignore the reasons and just honestly observe the behavior. (This is also part of developing emotional intelligence, a foundation for being a forward-thinking, progressive, and grounded person.) What conclusion would a casual observer draw from your behavior? Learn to notice the signs of self-sabotage. How and when do you do it? Be objective and recognize your patterns.

I offer you this word of caution and balance though. Remember that success isn't perfect. Sometimes we quit because things aren't turning out the way we imagined. Setting more reasonable expectations can help ensure that you're seeing things through to the end. Nothing in life is ever perfect. For instance, maybe you're in a great relationship, but you imagined there wouldn't be any disagreements. Or maybe you tried using a new process in your business, but you imagined there wouldn't be any hiccups or resistance. Those aren't practical expectations at all and remember that unrealistic expectations are exactly what fuels monsters that lead to becoming stuck or joyless.

This monster wants you to feel comfortable n being stuck, uninspired, and convinced that satisfaction comes from recycling and photocopying the past – even if it is hurting yourself and others.

It can be scary – believe me I do understand – but, before you throw in the towel, consider how it will affect those around you. That might provide enough motivation to continue pressing forward and being willing to be adventurous – responsibly, of course.

People who self-sabotage tend to stay in their own little worlds. Seeing a project through to completion means adjusting your outlook. Whether it's a different job, a new relationship, or something else, your life will be changed to a certain degree. Be brave enough to take that adventure.

If you are a hybrid – a person who prefers constancy and predictability, but you are also a highly imaginative person with lots of bright ideas – be mindful of tending to start new projects, but then stop yourself before ever completing them. That monster is waiting for the chance to push and pull you in various unclear directions, nothing will ever change, and you've just wasted time.

So, start small and give yourself the wonderful gift of having a few small successes. Then take the time to notice that these successes aren't perfect, but they still made your life better and enriched from them. Enjoy the victory and imagine how great it would be to accomplish greater successes.

Take some time before making any major decisions – remembering that others could be involved too. Before making a big decision, give yourself some time to think about it. Decisions can be impulsive. A few days can give you the perspective you require to make a wise decision.

Qualify and quantify your goals and your standards by constantly asking yourself "Why". Once you understand your motives and intentions, the "Why", then everything else should stem from it such as "How", "When", "Who", and "Where". Write down and break down your goals. I use the SMART method (Specific, Measurable, Achievable, Realistic and Time-Bound) to ensure that they are not too general nor too outrageous - which is a recipe for failure. Write down your top five personal values and revisit them weekly to see if you are still honoring yourself.

Next, remind yourself every day that time waits for no one. If you are a visual person, use a wall calendar that is "X'd" out daily, or sticky notes on your mirror, refrigerator, laptop. If you learn audibly, use your alarms, ask your accountability partner or life coach permission to record your motivation and action items that you can playback for yourself. Set time limits on watching entertainment on TV and social media – which often makes excuses for complacency and other self-sabotaging habit.

Finally, be ok with failure – success and growth are not possible without them. Your monster wants you to sulk and get stuck, nice a cozy, in failed attempts to stretch and grow. Self-forgiveness is as important as self-tough love. Remember that very few successes in life happen on the first attempt, or even the tenth attempt. As long as you learn, adjust, adapt, and be resolved you can achieve amazing things. Self-sabotage can be painfully frustrating. In the moment, it might seem like you're making a good choice, but eventually the truth becomes more apparent. It's easy to beat yourself up over your self-sabotaging behavior, but that can make it even harder for you to succeed the next time. Be good to yourself and avoid "shooting yourself in the foot" with self-sabotage. You can and will be successful!

See complacency for what it is – a monster. Go slay it!

AFFIRMATIONS

Being ambitious makes my life better.

I am blessed to possess ambition. When I think about everything I want in life like health, happiness, and a peaceful existence, I know that my level of ambition is integral to achieve those things.

To me, being ambitious is having energy, a sense of adventure, and a bold approach when it is needed.

Rather than wait for others to lead, I take responsibility to make things happen.

Showing ambition at work brings me many good things: respect from my co-workers, trust from my supervisor, and self-satisfaction regarding my career. The energy I demonstrate to others is motivating and encouraging to me and those around me.

My life has more variety because of my ambition.

SLAYING YOUR FEARS

In my personal life, I reach out to establish new relationships as opportunities arise. I agree to try new activities and explore different venues.

Each day, I strive to move forward and create the life I want. I realize that the existence I enjoy now is due to my ambitious endeavors.

Today, I know I can positively contribute to my life by showing ambition. I can assertively step forward and create the life I yearn for through my energy and adventuresome spirit.

SELF-REFLECTION QUESTIONS:

1. How ambitious am I? How do I demonstrate my ambition?
2. Reflecting back, when is the most recent time that I could have shown more ambition? How might I have been more ambitious then and what can I learn now from the situation?
3. What steps can I take each day to strengthen my ambition?

CHAPTER 2

THE MONSTER – MISPLACED LOYALTIES

"There's no point holding onto people who are holding you down, or who aren't holding you down. Read that again."

— Anonymous

WHY SLAY THIS FEAR

I USED TO HAVE AN OLD KEY RING that had about ten or so keys on it along with a dozen of those plastic frequent-shopper scanner key tags. To this day I still do not know to what doors or cabinets the keys unlocked despite asking loved ones or wracking my brain to remember.

For many years, every time I was doing spring cleaning, purging, or even moving this ring of keys and tags made an appearance and was given a new home in a drawer, on a hook, in a purse, or in my car's glove box. I am not a hoarder, so it was amazing that it managed to survive several junk cleanouts of my home. I am a huge germophobe, so it was struggle for me to deal the wear and tear of the old scanner tags. I also have an unnaturally heightened sense of smell so also struggled with the funky metallic scent of the keys. Despite those irritations, I pushed those negatives out of my mind and focused on the positive notion of hope that I would redeem their need and value – it was actually very funny. I had even taped up some of the worn-out tags which of course made it frustrating to scan at stores, defeating their purpose of convenience. I kept rationalizing that I, or someone, would be happy that I had that ring of keys in order to unlock something particularly important. I remember an annual cleanout project I had undertaken leading up to one New Year's Eve (I like having a totally cleaned home going into a new year). I had a few boxes packed and ready with old toys, books, and clothes. When I discovered that somehow that old key ring ended up in one of those boxes, I briefly gave in to a type of panic then relief. I chastised myself for being so clumsy; how could I be without something I had held onto for so long. I found a new home for it in my toolbox and determined to be more aware and try to remember their purpose – the locks they supposedly fit.

I began to select one-off memories to reinforce my fear, of occasions where I discarded an item only to feel regret afterwards, like an old earring, sock, or glove. As I finished my 'mental punishment', I comforted myself in remembering something about the key tags. Whoever found my key ring could have followed the instructions on them which says, "If found, please drop in any mailbox. Postage is guaranteed." My key ring would have been returned to me because I made it possible for that chance to exist. I kept hope alive and kept the proverbial "door open", just in case.

Another funny thing was that none of the keys were irreplaceable. They weren't the type of uncopiable keys such laser-cut, chip, transponder, or other types of restricted keys like PO Box or Safety Deposit Box. So, if I did in fact come face to face with the door or cabinet and did not have the old key ring, I could simply order a replacement key or hire a locksmith if necessary. It would have been a pain, but I will elaborate more about types of pain you experience when you're wrong, but still forcing your own way, later on.

Perhaps instead of an old key ring, you have had some piece of clothing that you continually move round in your closet year after year but never finding a reason or interest in wearing it; or a trinket or painting that gets placed on difference walls around your home but it just doesn't compliment your current décor or taste; a pair of shoes that are so fashionably sharp but incredibly uncomfortable; or a cooking pot with a missing handle or it constantly rusts.

Sometimes sentimentality, loyalty or nostalgia formulates reasons in our minds that convince us to hold onto and remain attached to things and people. They held a purpose, we assigned them a value, gave them a place, and allowed them to fill a need. In some ways they were part of our identity, language, rituals, appearance, and habits. To remove them and not hold onto them means we are disloyal, ungrateful, have a short memory, even wasteful.

I have had dresses that haven not been worn for years but remained in my closet. I have had decades-old trinkets and paintings in my home that I tried to make fit in the current décor. I have had a one-handle pot that, although causing a near accident while cooking, still found its way back into my cupboard. I have had fabulous custom- made stilettos that nearly tore foot muscles every time I wore them.

Eventually, I grew tired of the extra time, space, and pain I was causing myself. No one else was doing it to me and I knew it. Even though I liked the familiarity, ease, compliments, and style, I eventually donated the dresses, trinkets, paintings and stilettos and I tossed out the unrepairable and unsafe pot.

I also eventually tossed out that old key ring. Before doing so however, I cut up all the key tags as a further measure to prevent them somehow being returned to me, like a tormenting chain letter. To this day I haven't encountered any unopenable doors or cabinets and stores allow me to use my telephone number in lieu of scanner tags to get my coupons and savings. I had held onto something for so long, for the wrong reasons, and I created unnecessary mental punishment.

A monster that can be exceedingly difficult to slay, let alone face with complete honesty, is the fear of detachment. I am not speaking of the clinical fear that is rooted in a traumatic event and therefore warrants professional advice and services not provided in this book. The monster I specifically discuss in this chapter relates to personal and professional misplaced loyalties. This is the kind of loyalty to people, causes or even companies where your loyalty is not acknowledged, respected nor reciprocated. I'd also add that your values and beliefs nor longer align with theirs so loyalty or devotion to them comes into question. An additional likely factor is your loyalty is betrayed or taken advantage of in some way and often done repeatedly.

This monster behaves like a bratty, selfish, and sometimes mean child in some ways.

It likes to selfishly keep you in the past, attached to connections that weigh you down rather than uplift you. It likes to keep your eyes closed, blinded by false allegiance. It likes to keep your hands clenched and unable (or available) to receive a helping hand up or pull yourself up to your next level. Allow me to elaborate.

In today's world, we are always hearing about breakups, layoffs, dissolutions, or separations of some sort, ending with someone 'losing' and someone 'winning'. Think about your reaction when you last heard or read about someone breaking ties, changing sides, severing a relationship. Did you cynically accept it as norm, that regardless of what the causes could have been, all relationships – personal or professional - eventually end because people and agendas change anyway? Or were you saddened, appalled, disheartened, or even hopeful there would be a reconciliation, renewal of promises, mended fences, and a happy ending?

So, it is any wonder then, that this monster capitalizes on our natural desire to find and maintain strong and lasting relationships where loyalty is an essential component especially if there is a history, there is a past, you 'go way back'. Loyalty is becoming so rare and so sought after that it is one of the main subjects discussed – directly or indirectly – at job interviews or first dates. People and organizations judge character based on the longevity of relationships, looking at gaps and the role you played. If there weren't any gaps, they likely want to know why, what made that relationship so necessary, special, or different.

Loyalty is an important part of humanity – we like seeing this trait in action and we like to be on the receiving end. We even like to cheer for and celebrate the longevity of relationships we personally witness or hear about. We like the security and satisfaction of our own personal track record, that we are holding up our end, holding it down, part of a team, being the reliable 'ride or die', being the safety net, being the anchor, being the pillar. Because you have these admirable are rare traits, you have attracted one of two types of people to you. You have relationships with people who either mostly give or people who mostly take. Givers will have a true, proven, and current value and a necessary place in your life; they enhance, multiply and add to your assets, resources, and strengths. Takers will have inflated, antiquated, or imaginary reasons to be given room in your life (especially the front row); they force, divide, and subtract. Givers respect when your debts are paid, respect your boundaries, respect your forward momentum. Despite your debts being repaid or favors having been returned, takers will always want to find a way to collect interest from your life. They use guilt, blackmail, threats, or conveniently shadow or copy you in some way. Takers resort to a type of camouflaged bullying and shaming by referencing you to others as one of their examples of generosity or charity with their cloaked praise and flattery.

Your monster stomps into your life when it notices how you react to the takers. Your monster is ready to instigate internal turmoil when the takers disappoint you in some way by a lack a gratitude, a betrayal, indications of jealousy and possessiveness, theft, or an intrusion of your space and privacy. Your monster is fueled by what you allow, excuse, pardon, justify and remain silent about. Your monster thrives when you do not, disconnect, disassociate, delete, block, speak up, let go, or put distance between you and takers.

"Don't let your loyalty become slavery."

—Unknown

To be clear and realistic, everyone is a giver and a taker in some capacity. When in the role of a taker, when we need or want something, we seek it out and do what we can to get it. We use our knowledge of the situation, of ourselves and of the other individual to formulate our best possible argument in order to get what we want to accomplish our agenda. The leverage or ammunition we have could be secrets you share, the nature of the relationship (e.g., significant other, family member, business partner, friend, boss, investor, customer, benefactor, etc.), even knowledge of their weaknesses. In order to get more from to givers, takers need to regularly refresh and retain their presence in the life of the giver, reasserting their imagined value, otherwise their supply will run out and connection cut off. A supply of what? Time, attention, money, love, compliments, support, resources, connections, information, etc. Takers want to occupy space in your mind, heart, wallet, home, office, or life in some other way.

The value and satisfaction of our relationships, however, is weighed and measured by how much we gain and how much we lose.

Your monster, exploiting your desire to receive and demonstrate loyalty, convinced you that the takers could still have a place in your life, even though you constantly struggled for valid reasons why.

GET READY TO SLAY

AT TIMES, WE TAKE INVENTORY OF THE STATUS of our relationships and their merit. Your monster is relying on you to do this less and less. It wants you to hold space for non-essentials, for drainers of energy, for blockers of blessings, robbers of joy, saboteurs of happiness, thieves of peace, grabbers of resources, copies of originals, destroyers of progress. Your monster knows that misery loves company and takers are miserable. They thrive on keeping givers close to them, keeping them attached, committed, obligated, insecure, stuck and seemingly dependent. Givers need loyalty and takers cleverly capitalize on that neediness. This is a cycle with a very expense and exhausting toll. This toll comes in form of various types of precious currency like time, energy, peace, growth, reputation, creativity, and freedom. Is the toll that you pay worth it? Are you getting a fair return on your investment in the relationship or are you making more deposits than you are receiving dividends? Is the relationship depreciating in value year after year? Your monster is a deplorable 'adviser' pitching bad advice to you for a bad stock. Your monster is being enriched and fed but you are not. Let's put this into perspective.

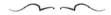

"Never make someone a priority when all you are to them is an option."
– *Maya Angelou*

No one is an island and there is no denying that relationships can be rewarding, satisfying and beautiful. In order for our world to be more united and resolve many of its problems, humanity still has far to go, and it starts with healthier relationships. By no means, therefore, am I advocating a life without attachments, being a cold, suspicious, antisocial recluse. This would be the opposite of living a full, enjoyable, and satisfying life and we would also lack essential traits like compassion, empathy, humility, patience, grace, and forgiveness. I want you to be aware, however, of the insidious nature of this monster and why it deserves to be slayed.

Let's talk about recognizing the warning signs of controlling relationships. You could be in a controlling relationship without even realizing it. Manipulative and dominating behavior can sometimes be subtle, but the effects are still deep.

Common warning signs include a person – friend, partner, relative, staff member, etc. - who tries to isolate you from your loved ones or your goals and often seems jealous and possessive. Their chronic criticism may whittle away at your self-esteem or you may feel pressured to stay on their good side because you know they're keeping score.

By contrast, healthy relationship makes you feel strong and supported.

If you suspect that your relationship may be tearing you down, consider these steps for turning things around and taking back your power. For starters, staying calm is key. Managing your emotions will help you to think rationally and stay in control. That way, you'll be able to deal with the facts of the situation instead of being lured or provoked into irrational behavior.

Always understand your options. Regardless of what the person does, you are in charge of your own decisions. Stick to your values and own your choices.

Keep your self-confidence high and of your own making. Give yourself a boost by reflecting on your talents and achievements. You are worthy of love just the way you are today.

As I covered in a previous chapter, don't rest on your laurels in complacency but keep pursuing your goals. Stand on your own two feet even if someone encourages you to totally depend on them. Make plans for your financial security and intellectual development. Devote your time and energy to projects you care about.

I especially encourage you to set boundaries. This was my biggest area to work on and hence, was the main way this monster was so effective in destroying my happiness, focus and management of my time. I'm going to linger on this a bit.

All relationships need boundaries to remain healthy. Boundaries help to determine how much you give and receive from a relationship.

If any of your relationships are leaving you irritable and overwhelmed, reexamine your boundaries.

Clarify your values and expectations. Define your limits so that you'll be able to communicate them and firmly stand by them.

Expand your horizons and circles by socializing and networking more. Hang onto your support system. Spend time with loving family and genuine friends on a regular basis.

The boundaries you set in your relationships reflect your ego and self-esteem so, if you have a low sense of self-worth, your boundaries are going to be unhealthy. You'll likely to be too focused on trying to please others and receive love and approval. You'll be overextending yourself and demanding too little from others. On the other hand, if your ego is over-inflated, your boundaries are aggressively set to maximize your own will - it's your way or the highway. For the healthiest and balanced results, seek middle ground when setting boundaries.

I learned the following strategies can help you set boundaries that are clear and empowering for everyone involved:

Make sure you are the one deciding your core values. What is your comfort level? Are you comfortable discussing your personal finances with others? Do you like friends or family just showing up at your front door or would you like a little warning? Are you willing to let others borrow your car, money, or clothes? How much honesty do you want to give and receive?

Determine what you need from the relationship. Communicate your needs to the other person in a healthy, non-blaming manner. This will require some measure of assertiveness on your part. It's not fair to expect anyone to read your mind and predict all of your wants and needs – do be clear, perhaps even writing your thoughts down in advance.

Now, at this point you want to consider determining the potential consequences. How will you handle it if someone violates your boundaries? Remind others of your boundaries and then take prompt action. It someone shows up unannounced, for example, don't let them in your home, as was agreed. If you offered a one-time free consultation with a new client to pick your brain, for example, make sure an invoice is sent and paid before additional consulting calls are done. If you want to attend an event by yourself rather than take a best friend, for example, make sure this is made clear while offering whatever reassurances are needed.

I was a devout people-pleaser so at times I lacked firmness. So here is where I encourage you to be consistent. It's natural for others to test you when you change the rules. It's important to be consistent, or you won't be taken seriously. Follow through and keep your word. One slip into your old patterns and you'll probably have a battle on your hands.

Reality may hit hard though, and you have to be prepared to let go. It's likely that some individuals will keep on behaving the same way, regardless of your efforts. If a person is unable or unwilling to appreciate your boundaries and requirements, it might be best to reexamine the relationship. Redefining a relationship can be challenging and stressful. Change isn't always popular. When people can no longer take advantage of you, you're sure to experience some resistance. But when you maintain your efforts consistently, you and those around you will all ultimately benefit.

Take a pause and objectively evaluate your situation. Ask yourself how your relationship is affecting your life. Maybe your relationship is worth working on or maybe it's time to move on. Be willing to walk away if your wellbeing is being compromised.

A controlling person may be trying to cover up their own insecurities. Reassure them by demonstrating your commitment and trustworthiness. Develop rituals that draw you closer together, like shared hobbies and in-depth conversation. If, however you feel that the conversations are mostly one-sided, let them know that you enjoy listening to them, but you need to share too.

By all means never gloss over continual and habitual conflicts - face them. I can't overstate this. If a controlling relationship is wearing you down, you may feel like it's safer to stay silent and avoid disagreements. Unfortunately, that will cause more resentments and misunderstandings. Try to resolve your conflicts respectfully instead.

Remember the importance of assertiveness which includes bring an issue to proper focus with the intent on a resolution – this means you'll need to switch the focus at times. There is an alternative to being scrutinized and criticized. If you think they are is trying to blame you, change the conversation around to examine their contribution to the situation too – with specifics, not generalizations. Even better, team up on finding solutions that satisfy both of you.

Of course, I'm going to recommend seeking counseling, management input, coaching, or a spiritual advisor. If you're having trouble making progress on your own, joint counseling may help. You can also benefit from seeing a therapist on your own if the person resists.

Unhealthy relationships can sneak up on you. Learning to spot the warning signs will help you avoid controlling patterns and develop a balanced and loving connection that reinforces your self-esteem.

But what about avoiding personal or professional relationships that sap your soul? It's easy to get drawn into a negative relationship. It may have started out seemingly perfect, but things seemed to change overnight. It may be time to decide whether or not the positive attributes outweigh the negative ones when it comes to your relationship choices.

If you're unhappy and emotionally drained after a breakup or a business partnership fail, you might not be feeling too optimistic about throwing yourself back out there. However, opening yourself up to new opportunities is the only way you're going to reach the happiness you seek.

The best thing you can do is to educate yourself well enough to know what to look for and what to avoid. It's not a fail-proof plan, but by following certain strategies, you can increase your chances of better relationships.

Avoid falling back on the wrong person. If you're feeling particularly lonely, you may feel the urge to fall back on someone that's not right for you. Deep down you know that this person is not "the one" and yet you come crawling back anyway trying to convince yourself that maybe the person can change. Chances are, they won't.

Spend time getting to know the person first – vetting, due diligence, interviews, trial arrangement, etc. Focus on getting to know them first before getting too serious in the relationship or commitment. Try to have some of the heavy conversations near the beginning of the relationship. This way if you hit major snags you can either decide to work through it or move on quickly.

Are there disturbing events in his or her past? It's clearly best to avoid people who have a history of violence or intense addiction. If they do and you choose to proceed with the relationship, be extra cautious and set the ground rules from the beginning.

Avoid manipulative people. You might not realize it at first, but if you find that you're being manipulated often, it can prove to be a serious drain on your relationship. If they are controlling and always has a selfish motive for their actions – even if it is a professional relationship - it isn't the best relationship to be in. Recognize these red flags when you see them and get out before you get too attached.

Know what you want and make a basics checklist. Take some time to make a list of the qualities you'd like to see in a partner, friend, manager, business partner. Include qualities you like as well as qualities that you dislike. This checklist will help you determine whether the relationship is right for you.

Relationships can be difficult; it's just a reality of human nature. The fact that many relationships end shouldn't have any impact on your hope for the future. There are plenty of people out there that will be a good match for you personally and professionally, so it's okay to avoid relationships that sap your soul.

I've had the unfortunate experience of feeling a friendship was one-sided even though I felt compelled to maintain my loyalty to it. I felt I was constantly scooping seawater out of boat full of holes in it. Trying to keep the boat afloat was becoming futile, depressing, infuriating, and exhausting.

Many friendships are a bit lopsided sometimes. However, if things remain out of balance for too long, you may want to fix the situation or go your separate ways. One-sided friendships come in many varieties, but they have one thing in common. You supply most of the effort, while your friend is distant or does things that actually hurt you. In the end, you wind up lacking the support and companionship you deserve.

Healthy friendships are important to our social and mental wellbeing so, you can and should make room in your life for healthy relationships where you'll feel cared for and appreciated.

Because misplaced loyalties and overstretched expectations usually occur within friendships, try these tips for recognizing and dealing with one-sided friendships so that you can make room for the happier and more fulfilling relationships you desire.

Take time off. If your friendship is already strained, it may help to distance yourself for a while. You're likely to think more clearly after you take a break.

Expand your network. While you're sorting things out, you can take advantage of opportunities to hang out with other friends and make new contacts. Expecting too much from any single relationship can put too much and unfair pressure on both of you.

Expect change. Friendships evolve. Maybe you started out feeling close, but you've been drifting in opposite directions. Evaluate your current lifestyle and values to see what makes sense for you now.

Consider counseling. If one-sided friendships seem to be a pattern for you, it may help to talk with a therapist. Working with a professional could give you new insights and coping strategies.

Clarify the situation. Distinguish between a friend who seems distracted and one who is abusive or deceptive. Talk with your friend to see if your perceptions are accurate. They may have a different perspective on your relationship.

This one is my favorite and created a huge turning point for me in having better relationships with others - Advocate for yourself. Speak up for yourself! Let your friend know what you need. Be specific without being judgmental. Tell them if it bothers you to be kept waiting when they're late for coffee dates. Let others know when you're going through difficult times and need more assistance than usual.

Exchange information. You can reduce your risk of one-sided friendships by taking the time to build a solid foundation for your relationships. Engage in mutual and gradual disclosure, so you really get to know each other from a clearer vantage point.

Share support. Similarly, pay attention to whether you both rally around to prop each other up during challenging times and celebrate happy occasions. Your friend's past track record can help you predict if they'll be there for you when you need them.

Follow through. If you want your friend to be reliable and considerate, show them the same courtesy. Keep your word if you promise to plan a party together or drive them to the airport.

Stay in touch. It often happens that one friend reaches out more frequently. You'll need to decide if this makes your friendship unfulfilling or if it's just a minor difference that you can live with. See what happens if you let your friend know that you'd appreciate more initiative on their part.

Be patient. If your friend is dealing with a divorce or other hardships of their own, they may be less available temporarily. Consider what's going on in their life before making any major decisions.

Move on. On the other hand, you both may benefit from time apart if you feel like you're being taken for granted. Recognizing your incompatibility will probably be less stressful than allowing resentments to grow.

Say goodbye to one-sided friendships. Boost your health and happiness by developing mutually supportive relationships based on give and take. Remember: you do have a choice! Focus on finding the right people for you and then take action to make it the positive relationship you've always dreamed of!

AFFIRMATIONS

I am strong enough to let others know what I need.

Part of my strength is my ability to speak out and make my wishes known. I speak out in a way that is gentle, but assertive. I am strong enough to let others know what I need.

My needs are important, and I am willing to accept help to fulfill them.

I understand that it is difficult for others to give me what I require if I fail to inform them of my needs. I am comfortable letting people know what I want from them. I encourage them to do the same. I like to help others, and they like to help me.

Sometimes, I might be too embarrassed to let someone know my wishes. But then I remember that admitting I have desires is really a display of my strength, and people admire others that show strength.

SLAYING YOUR FEARS

I am becoming more and more comfortable with making requests. We could all do more to help each other - it is a form of bonding. I am free of anxiety when asking for assistance.

I feel more confident, assertive, and proud when I make my needs known.

Today, I am letting the world know what I require from it. I assist others with their needs and expect the same in return. I am supporting someone else as much I wish to be supported.

SELF-REFLECTION QUESTIONS:

1. What unmet needs do I have in my life?
2. Who could I ask to help me with these needs?
3. Is there a relationship I am maintaining that is causing me distress or harm?

CHAPTER 3

THE MONSTER – INDECISIVENESS

"Most of the problems in life are because of two reasons: we act without thinking or we keep thinking without acting."

— *Anonymous*

When I was younger, I was envious of the girls who could jump double-dutch rope. They always looked so cool, in control and happy doing their rhythmic routines, while popping their gum, and singing jump rope songs as the two ropes slapped the ground, quickly whirred over their head and under their dancing feet. Their talent was judged not only by how long they could jump without the ropes hitting their feet, but they were also judged by their 'choreographed' routines that included certain dances to specific songs or ad-libbed fancier gymnastic-style tricks to impress onlookers. And impress they did. Not only was the girl who owned a double-dutch rope (it was usually just a clothing line) considered one of the neighborhood queens but the girls who knew how to jump double-dutch were like her entourage of consorts – the cool group of talented, high stepping, gum popping, choreographed fabulousness.

Seeing a few ladies jumping double-dutch is still a staple at many family cookouts today, seen on school recess yards, and there are still a few competitive national double-dutch leagues even featuring multiple jumpers within the ropes at a time while performing amazing moves - never missing a step.

When I was younger, I would beg the neighborhood girls to let me try to jump but year after year I was ignored or designated the "baby doll" and only allowed to jump regular single jump rope for the "babies". You see, I could not jump double-dutch (nor could I turn the double-dutch ropes very well either). Sometimes I would be given a pity lesson to practice and get used to the two ropes, but time and again I just could not master it.

My problem wasn't that I was shy or lacked rhythm. In fact, I could simulate the dance steps outside of the jump ropes fine even doing some of the complex hand to foot slapping jumping tricks. My problem was that it took me far too long to jump into the ropes and get going – as if I were mentally frozen. As the double ropes would turn I hemmed and hawed, back, and forth, hovering and hesitating to just jump in. I hesitated so much so that the girls would often get frustrated with me, forgo my turn, and make me wait to try again another time. Sometimes a girl would offer to count me off and push me in or sometimes I would do a running start. It was actually pretty hilarious because I would often freeze up and come to a full halt instead of just making the choice to jump rope. It seemed like the easiest thing – just step forward and jump in. I had no real reason to be scared and embarrassed after all, many of the girls were at different levels, some being more advanced than others. Sometimes I would make it in through the ropes and make it for a few moments and other times it was a failure. Unfortunately, because I got in my own head by constantly hesitating, I missed out on opportunities to just have fun, be creative and possibly getting better. I turned a trivial activity into a prolonged frustration not only for me but for others as well. Those who simply wanted to jump rope either waited for me to decide or were compelled to just push me into a decision.

Being indecisive when it came to jumping double-dutch was likely the result of a slowly developing monster rooted in perfectionism, insecurity, being overwhelmed and self-doubt. Indecisiveness is a challenging monster to contend with not only because of how clever it operates but because it has numerous methods effective in causing disruption and delay in your life. Let's look at a few.

When I first heard the term 'analysis paralysis', I wasn't fully aware of the powerful truth of that phrase. At that time, I was convinced that being an overthinker, being a "what if" person, being a doubter with endless speculation and pessimism was an asset and guaranteed high success and low disappointment because I'd mentally consume myself with every possible scenario or outcome. This thinking not only prevented me from enjoying a childhood pastime like double-dutch but robbed me of peace and limited my movements in other ways.

It was hard for me to relate to people who are impulsive, reactive, or impetuous because they frequently seemed to always be involved in unravelling or undoing something they'd jumped into and although I was secretly admiring them, I didn't feel confident to jump as they did. For me, on the other hand, it seemed that Murphy's Law liked to make an example of me whenever I tried to ignore my monster, my fear by daring to leap into the deep end without thought or hesitation. When this happened it sometimes ruined my creativity, stifled my curiosity, and built defensive walls that made me not only question myself but also mistrust others who I felt were too pushy or too eager.

Self- doubt, self-berating and self-deprecating thoughts are some of the worst aspects of this monster to contend with because of the constant battle to strike a balance of

acting with fearlessness and vacillating in caution. On the one hand we want our lives to feel enriched, varied, challenging and meaningful but indecisiveness chokes creativity, ambition, and open-mindedness. But unfortunately, indecisiveness can also give the impression you are wishy-washy, disloyal, or unqualified. In recent years, the term imposter syndrome has given rise to individuals who are professionally qualified and equipped but they suffer with self-doubt and will recoil or reject opportunities to shine their own light, because they compare themselves to others who are more prominent, who are louder, and who seem to have the Midas Touch in all they do.

You likely realize that this monster did not just appear out of nowhere and began to make its first appearances in your life long ago. Although I can't pinpoint exactly when this monster came into existence for me, I realized that seemingly simple activities like jumping double-dutch was an indicator of this monster's formative years within me.

Another face this monster wears in order to deceive you and trigger your indecisiveness occurs when you seem to have multiple plausible options to choose from and endless time to do so. Some scenarios can include situations such as: A decision to stand in your truth and beliefs when under pressure or to retreat. Perhaps juggling several romantic interests, or entertaining numerous employment offers is an accomplishment and means you can write your own ticket.

Having multiple options to pick from is not the problem and can be a good thing to compare or reaffirm your preferences and needs. The challenge is understanding the reasons for your indecision and hesitation.

For instance, when you're feeling the angst and pressure of an approaching or overdue deadline, or because you prefer to operate at your own slower, deliberate, and cautious pace to weigh options, you become hesitant to act unless you can deliver perfection and preferably the first time around.

Or, due to paralyzing relationships with overbearing, critical, smothering, ambiguous, or opinionated people you may be inclined to dodge and avoid them, prolonging your input, or resigning and deferring to other's.

Or, perhaps crippled with shame you haven't forgiven yourself for past mistakes – injury caused to yourself or to others – you avoid certain decisions not fully trusting yourself or assuming that you won't be trusted (guilt will be covered more in the last chapter).

Hesitation in these situations and others gave birth to that oppressive monster that keeps pushing you to the back of the line missing and your turn, backward into a corner of inactivity or silent resignation in the hopes that your decisions will be made for you or, if you do make them there is little disruption in your life or attention brought to you. This can sabotage you personally as friendships and interests may lose patience or trust with your ability to act with confidence, honesty, or clarity. Also, potentially in jeopardy are your professional prospects.

Many employers, business partners or clients hire, retain, and endorse their professionals who are resolute, intrepid self-starters and exhibit confidence rather than indecisiveness.

Regret is one of the many deflating and frustrating emotions we'll experience in life. Hearing our inner voice screaming "shoulda, coulda, woulda" as we recap and relive the reasons we didn't speak up, stand up or act sooner is its own form of torture this monster dumps on us, and sadly we often suffer in silence trying to determine when and how this monster will make its appearance again and if we'll miss out on

yet another opportunity. But where to start?

GET READY TO SLAY

CAN YOU SEE THE JOY-ROBBING CYCLE OF THIS FEAR and its devastating effects on your life? Not only does this monster cause a waste of time and other precious resources, but it can also slowly allow other little nasty monsters to creep into your life including jealousy, resentment, and exhaustion. This happens to many people when they are faced with the realization of how their life is lacking true joy, passion, or peace resulting from ineffective decision-making. So, let's look at how to end indecisiveness once and for all.

When you own your decisions, you own yourself. You live by your values and stop wavering back and forth over matters big and small, whether it's buying a house or ordering breakfast. You take control of your future instead of turning the responsibility over to someone else.

Effective decision-making is a skill that you can polish even if you've had trouble making up your mind in the past. Here's how you can say goodbye to feeling frustrated and mater the decision-making process:

Remember your purpose. Think about the essence of who you are and what you want to achieve. Align your choices with your values.

Gather your information. Having an accurate and up-to-date picture of your situation will help you to know what to do. However, research can drag on so long that it becomes a form of procrastination, as I covered in another chapter, so put a time limit on it.

Clarify your options. Consider each of your possible choices. You usually have several reasonable alternatives to compare, even if they're new or unusual, rather assuming there's only one or none.

Weigh different factors. Some items are bound to be more important to you than others. For example, you might compare two job offers by writing down all the criteria and assigning numbers to them so you can see the one with the highest score based on salary, commute time, and other considerations. Or you may do the same when deciding on a business partner that you are vetting.

Make a commitment. Select your favored option and let it sink in. Once you have a clear winner, let go of the temptation to keep rehashing, rethinking and reevaluating other scenarios. I am a "what if" person myself so this step was hard for me, but I eventually noticed the time and opportunities that eluded me and some of my relationships that became strained because of it.

Move forward. Put your decision into action. Do what you can to make it work.

Evaluate your progress. Remember that most decisions are at least somewhat reversible. Scheduling regular time to analyze the outcomes will help you enjoy your victory or make some modifications.

If you're thinking that it will take time to become a more decisive person, you're absolutely right. Yes, there will be obstacles; however, consider some additional helpers that I've learned while slaying this fear myself:

Slow down. Avoid acting on impulse or creating unnecessary pressure on yourself to pick an option when you still feel unsure. You may see things more clearly when you sleep on a decision or talk it over with someone you trust.

Listen to your feelings. Your gut and your emotions often tell you what you really value. Pay attention if an otherwise reasonable choice causes anxiety for you or a less conventional route makes you smile.

Reassess your choices. It's possible to have too many options and wind up overwhelmed especially if these options came to you under rushed pressure, such as an approaching deadline. Narrow the field down even more perhaps including professional input, before making a final decision.

Distance yourself and take a step back. Imagine what advice you'd give to someone else in the same circumstances. It's often a quick way to persuade yourself to think more objectively.

Accept trade-offs. What if several options offer different advantages? At some point, you may have to let something go to gain the things you want more – as long as you honor your core values and macro goals.

Achieve consensus. Be careful with this one though, to avoid time waste and inaction. Some decisions affect more than one individual and need to be shared. For example, your advisory board, business partner, family, spouse or

Look inward. Confirm that you're making decisions for yourself instead of following the crowd or trying to please someone else. Your happiness depends on listening to your heart. Your definition of fulfillment and success is what counts.

Indecisiveness can lead to frustration, wasted time, and lost opportunities. Free yourself from excessive doubts and second-guesses. Choose your course and move forward even when the stakes are high, uncomfortable, or scary. Either the results will turn out in your favor, or you can learn from the experience and make the necessary adjustments.

"Being brave isn't the absence of fear. Being brave is having that fear but finding a way through it."

— Anonymous

I do understand that this slaying this monster is a challenge when you continually worry about failure – the very feelings that keep you stuck and hesitant. But the problem is that this fear of failure can in fact become one of your biggest life fears.

Fear of failure is a fear of the great unknown. You don't know what's truly out there, and so you're scared. You might even be tempted to give up entirely in order to avoid failure. You'll soon realize that not trying at all is the ultimate failure because there is no way to win without trying.

How can you get out of this loop of frustration, overcome this fear, and gain the confidence you need to achieve the life you desire?

Imagine the worst-case scenario. Remember, this is the premise of this book! Of course, you should spend time imagining everything turning out well, but it actually helps to imagine the worst case as well, with the correct objective. This is because, while horrible, imagining the worst case gives your fears a face. Your fears monsters are then no longer the unknown and they may not be quite as big and undefeatable.

When you figure out the worst thing that can happen, you just might realize that the most a failure can do is to delay your ultimate goal. But if you can figure out how to get past this possible delay, you're back on track! Take bold action. The fear of failure can hold you hostage. When you take bold action, you're able to learn from your mistakes so you can continuously move forward.

Talk to and surround yourself with successful people. Ask them about times that they've failed or times that they've felt a fear of failure. It's likely that they were afraid too and that they've even failed greatly before reaching success. Knowing that you're not alone can be quite helpful.

Utilize affirmations. If you've read some of my other writings, you likely anticipated me eventually suggesting this to you. Use the help of affirmations in order to change your mindset about your fears. Affirmations can help you reprogram your subconscious mind so that you believe you'll succeed, which will encourage you to take action to make it happen.

Believe and know that you'll try again. Tell yourself that, if you're face to face with failure, you will pick yourself up and you will try again no matter how many tries it takes. Then follow your plan.

Don't be afraid of help. Since the fear of failure is so common, there are many people around you that you can selectively talk to about the subject. You might feel like you're alone, but you're not. Discuss your issues with a trusted friend or use the services of a professional counselor. Sometimes just having someone listen and understand you

– not to enable you nor make your decisions for you - can make your fears seem like less of a burden. It can help you to get into a positive mindset, which is the first step you'll need to take in order to tackle your fear of failure head-on.

After you've mastered your fear of a particular situation – which may likely take time depending how large and deeply rooted it is - keep at it in order to stay on top of your fears. The key is consistency and positive thoughts. Remember that there are always lessons to be learned on your journey, even if you've failed. Keep at it and good things will come!

Conquering self-doubt and becoming more self-confident is very possible for you and is necessary for slaying this monster. Self-doubt is what kept me hesitant to "jump in the ropes" and enjoying new experiences even if I failed a few times.

Everyone has times in their life when they feel inadequate and incompetent, but some of us feel that way more often than others. Many people are so busy putting themselves down they fail to thrive in life. They stop trying to learn and better themselves. They become discouraged and depressed. Do you feel like you may be one of these people?

Maybe your self-doubt stems from some negative experiences early in your life. For example, if people made fun of you when you were a child, you might doubt your abilities even today. Traumatic experiences can cause a vicious cycle of self-doubt in your mind.

Parents, teachers, and other children can sometimes unwittingly say things that have a powerful impact for both good and bad and can last in your psyche for an exceptionally long time. So, how do you turn things around and stop that nagging voice in your head that says you'll never be good enough?

Here are some tactics to help you erase that doubt and become more confident:

Let go of negative criticism of yourself. This applies to both past and present. Don't let a jerk of a boss ruin your day by simply adding his voice to the tape player in your head and loudly repeating itself. Realize that he may be taking his anger out on someone else – projecting - because of his own inadequacies. People's negative attitudes speak volumes about them, not about you!

Stifle your tendency to criticize yourself. By agreeing with those who criticize you, you're giving them all the power.

Pay no attention to that voice in your head that's saying you're going to fail. If you stop listening, it will get quieter and eventually disappear- especially if you utilize positive affirmations, as I previously covered. Reclaim your life by believing that you CAN succeed.

Surround yourself with supportive people who believe in you. Remember misery loves company so don't RSVP to partake in conversations (live or virtual) with people or groups that fuel the monster you're trying to slay.

Prepare yourself and do your best. It's not enough just to think positively; you have to actively pursue success as well. Visualizing your end goal can help you make the right choices but remember that no one can do the work except you.

One way to overcome self-doubt is to write down your positive qualities in your journal, on your vision board, or your cell phone's home screen, or even make an audio recording of a love note to yourself that you can listen to for a pep talk power boost – I still do this! Make a list of at least five good things about you. Every day when you wake up read the list. Reading aloud will also help you to believe the items you've listed.

The positive thinking will help prepare your mind to succeed, but there are other ways you can help yourself achieve your goals as well.

Set reasonable goals. I've previously mentioned goal setting but I want to reinforce this essential part of your battle armor, if you will, because it will protect you in many ways. Decide what you want to do within a set amount of time. Keep your goals realistic so you can meet them. If you set unrealistic goals that you can't meet, you'll quickly become discouraged. Start out small and get bigger with your dreams.

Get busy. Inactive people easily become depressed. To avoid this unpleasant situation, immerse yourself in achieving your goals. Hard work will always pay off in the end.

Savor and revel in your success. Self-doubters tend to think they don't deserve to succeed. But you do! You deserve a reward for conquering your self-doubt and becoming more confident. You deserve to be honored for your hard work and perseverance. Don't let anyone tell you otherwise.

Just remember you can't reach the top of a mountain in one giant leap; it takes many steps along the way to reach the peak in due time. The same is true of success and achieving your goals. Dig in, turn the tables, and use fear to your advantage:

Determine why you're afraid. If for example, it's just your ego or pride talking, you know that the fear isn't in your best interests. That's the fear that keeps you in your current situation.

Reframe the situation. The fact that you're feeling things like awkwardness, pressure, or uncomfortable doesn't have to control your thoughts or actions. When you're feeling anxious, take that as a sign that something great might be getting ready to happen. Step outside your comfort zone and take advantage of the opportunity and decide. Use your fear to your advantage. It's a good thing, not something to be avoided. Embrace it.

Make a more specific list of when this fear makes an appearance. You'll notice a pattern. It might be a fear of embarrassment, success, or becoming isolated. By understanding the core of your fears, you can better deal with them and eliminate many of them at the source.

Use fear to propel you forward. The most successful people have been those that faced fear successfully even if it took multiple attempts to slay it. Conquering one fear makes you more capable. The next fear will be even easier. Defeating a small fear makes the more significant fears more manageable. The confidence you gain can be applied to all areas of your life.

Use this fear to enhance your discipline. Fear occurs when your brain tries to stop you from doing something. It makes you uncomfortable until you run away from the source of your fear. Use the opportunity to exercise your ability to push through the back and forth of indecisiveness. Discipline is the ability to do things you don't feel like doing. You don't need discipline to do the things you enjoy. Taking baby steps and attaining many small successes will bring you the confidence to reach your dreams. In the meantime, sit back and enjoy the journey to becoming the self-assured person you know you can be. It's definitely a tricky and sometimes wild ride, but it's well worth it in the end.

Finally, remember that your thoughts are what you can control in life, even if there are external variables that you can't control. I learned that it was me was breathing life into self-destructive thoughts keeping me paralyzed and stuck and the following are some tips banishing negative self-destructive thoughts that I still need to remind myself of everyday.

Do you notice when negative, self-destructive thoughts creep into your mind? Are you sending yourself these troubled messages? Let's look at some examples that you may be able to relate to, and suggestions for slaying this monster:

Let's say you're hesitating because of fearing you're being judged or that no one understands you. If you feel this way pause, and quickly make note of those that do love and support you – friends, family members, and co-workers – and you'll realize that there are indeed people who accept you and "get" you. As I've always said: I may not be everyone's cup of tea but I'm someone's glass of whiskey. Every will always have an opinion, but your happiness shouldn't hinge on it as long as you're making effort to improve yourself as a human being.

Maybe you feel you don't have enough time to experiment or deviate from the norms you're accustomed to and talk yourself out of taking action to challenge anyone – including yourself. If the only things you have time to do are things you have to do or have been strictly comfortable with doing it sure doesn't make life very fulfilling or event profitable.

Begin working to achieve a healthy balance in your life. Allow time each day to take part in things that make your heart sing. Start small, if you need to, by scheduling just 15 minutes for yourself for introspection and reflection on how you can assertively take action to enrich yourself, make yourself more desirable, adaptable, marketable, visible, relatable, and reliable. When you proactively take control of your decision making, and when you better manage your schedule, evaluate your options, you'll gain confidence and also build a track record of actively progressing toward doing what you want to do.

Another self-sabotaging mindset that keeps you from living with decisiveness is telling yourself that you don't deserve to be happy. Perhaps choices you've made in the past have caused you considerable pain and you've been beating yourself up over those decisions, and in doing so crippling your confidence in making decisions. However, if you've identified them as poor choices, you've learned not to repeat them. Congratulate yourself for learning from your mistakes. You've gained new knowledge to use from this day forward. Be determined to face this monster, confront this type of thinking by saying, "No, this negative thought isn't right. I do deserve to have a happy life. After all, I learn well from my mistakes."

Another symptom of what I call "stinkin'-thinkin'" is truly defeatist and corrodes your confidence and decision making. Statements like, "Things never seem to work out for me" or, "Why should I even make a move?" are a general statement that colors how you feel about yourself. It sends a subtle self-message: "I must not be doing anything right." I can empathize with the reasons for being overtaken by this monster. When you've taken risks or leaps of faith that didn't yield the results you hope it likely hurt you or cost you in some way – financially, emotionally, spiritually, or even physically.

Listen! In reality, you likely do many things well. Spend some time identifying what those things are. Also, you may be focusing too much on what doesn't work out well and barely noticing what's going right in your life. Take time now to write down what you do well.

Remember though the danger of succumbing to that nemesis monster, perfection by saying things like, "If I can't do it perfectly, then I'm not doing it at all." It's wonderful that you want to do your best in all that you do. But how will you try anything new if it has to be done perfectly? How will you make solid and firm decisions if the circumstances have to be perfectly carved out? Thinking this way will prevent you from ever venturing outside your comfort zone.

Try adopting a new mantra: "If at first I don't succeed; I'll keep trying until I do." Allow yourself the opportunity to make mistakes. Remind yourself that making a mistake is a real learning experience you can benefit from. Optimistically embrace your errors and move forward.

If you're still finding yourself apprehensive and saying, "I'm afraid to do the things I really want to do", what are you specifically afraid of? What is the face of the monster – so you can know what you're fighting? The source of your fears could likely be embarrassment, failure, or what others will think. In reality, it's healthy to have a certain amount of fear when embarking upon something new or unknown.

The key is that, even though you feel the fear, you must do the thing you want to do anyway. Otherwise, you'll never know what positive things could happen as a result of your following through with your hopes and dreams.

When negative thoughts begin to invade your mind, nip them in the bud with the above suggestions. Banish your self-destructive thoughts forever and live a life filled with joy and serenity. After all, you deserve it!

AFFIRMATIONS

I am a flexible thinker.

I embrace the depth of my mind. I am encouraged by the thoughts I generate.

I challenge my mind to produce creative thoughts and ideas. When I take this approach, I end up with many possible options. My ideas show that I am a flexible thinker.

In group situations when there is a matter to be resolved, I confidently play my part in coming up with the solution. I know that even if my suggestions may be unsuitable, it may inspire other suggestions. I am happy to be a part of the decision-making process.

My flexibility helps make life easier for others. I do my best to help whenever I can. When I am able to ease someone else's burden, I feel happy.

There are times when a situation is unfavorable to me. At these times, I think of ways to rectify things with minimal fallout. I try to make the best of whatever I am presented with.

I consider the pros and cons of every decision. That tactic helps me make informed decisions. It prevents me from coming to hasty conclusions, which can be damaging.

Today, I challenge myself to be flexible in my thinking. I am committed to believing in the silver lining. I know there is usually an alternate choice. I am confident that my creative thinking can produce viable solutions.

SELF-REFLECTION QUESTIONS:

1. How can I display flexible thinking and still be decisive?
2. What can I do to respectfully challenge the opinion of others if I believe there is a better way?
3. How can I ensure that I am satisfied with my decisions?

CHAPTER 4

THE MONSTER – GUILT

"Guilt is rooted in actions of the past, perpetuated in the lack of action in the present, and delivered in the future as pain and suffering."

— David Roppo

I don't have a relationship with my mother. Yes, she is alive and well; however, I made the personal decision some years ago to sever contact with her. Now, some reading this may raise an eyebrow and begin to formulate all sorts of questions in your minds. Since I'm placing this personal experience in a chapter addressing guilt, allow me to elaborate on a few attitudes and behaviors – both positive and negative – that resulted from this decision and may help you to have insight regarding the status of your relationships, their purpose, their impact on your ability or inability to achieve happiness.

For over thirty years, my relationship with my mother was a constant emotional tug of war. This was due to manipulation, abuse, deceit, and selfishness I'd experienced. There was no lack of conversations, family meetings, confrontations, counselling, tears and hurt that plagued me for a long time. I wanted to have what many other women had – a healthy, affectionate, and loving bond with my mother while completely understanding that neither of us are perfect. I was in a cycle of confrontation, confusion, reconciliation, betrayal, forgiveness, harshness and lying year after year that eventually she alienated herself from everyone time again. There was no one situation that broke the proverbial camel's back, but I had to acknowledge and accept that she was not capable of having a lasting relationship with anyone and I could no longer endure the damage it was causing me – and the damage was so severe that it took years missteps I had made with female authority figures, unresolved questions regarding my own personal identity, needs, preferences and much of this I had to work through in counseling.

There is a popular saying, that sometimes you have to simply love a person at a distance, and not hold a front row seat for them in your life. For me, when I made my final decision to 'cut her off' I did not feel sad or grieved but I felt I did the responsible thing in order to protect the quality of my life and preserve my happiness.

Of course, some well-meaning people would advise that no one should cut off their mothers – their life givers - and that I should be grateful that mine is alive since there are those who have lost their mothers and grieve their own loss, and that I would feel incredible guilt for choosing not having a relationship with mine.

Of course, there were occasions too numerous to even mention, where I did have a natural longing for the affection, conversation, connection, and loving memories that one would expect to have with their mother. For instance, every Mother's Day I would envy the photos others would share boasting of the fun and traditional outings with their mothers and the friendship they'd enjoyed. I would even envy those who mourned their mothers during this time as they recounted pleasant stories of the wisdom and lessons they still treasured. I would feel a sense of awkwardness when I was asked why I spoke so much and affectionately about my fathers but not about my mother.

Happily, I was able to develop great relationships with mother-figures and that allowed me to enjoy the refreshment, wisdom and security that should exist in healthy relationships. Once I realized that guilt is like rust to your soul, I learned to see guilt as an enemy and true barrier to happiness.

The thing about the monster guilt is that it's a trap - much like a sticky one at that - because not only does it catch you, but it's extremely hard to pull it off of you and not carry it around. This is what I came to eventually realize once I decided to identify, create, and protect the kind of life I wanted to have and knew I deserved.

All of us have decisions to make in our lives – major or minor. For some of these, they are common, we can foresee them, they could be easier to plan for, manage, and even receive support to deal with their consequences – good or bad. Other decisions we face, however, are unusual, sudden, or compound and complex issues where the answers are not so cut-and-dry, are based on an individual's conscience, and are a private matter so we may be completely on our own to figure it out.

Let's consider some of these examples, and why this monster thrives and blocks your happiness when you aren't resolved or confident in your decisions or you are plagued by guilt once you've made them.

There's no shortage of opinions you'll hear or read about when it comes to who you 'should' or 'should not' date, marry, divorce, if you 'should' or 'should not' choose to have children, maintain a relationship with someone who deeply wronged or hurt you, or if you 'should' or 'should not' start a business, end a friendship, have a medical procedure, where to worship, and so on. Most of us couldn't wait to be 'grown' and live our own lives, and no problem asserting our independence and telling people to mind their own business when it came to our own choices. For others, the comfort and assuredness of making decisions isn't as easy because of consequences experienced in the past. Sometimes the results of our decisions may have brought gratification, quiet, peace, healing, wealth, or release, and other times they may have brought ostracization from a church, a circle of friends or family, removal from a professional position, shaming, ridiculing or judgement on social media, loss of clients or other scenarios that involved some sort of loss.

When our decisions had less than the desired effects our confidence takes a hit and our stride toward progress gets stalled. This can happen to anyone at any age, career level, business acumen, social visibility, or education level. Enter – the monster guilt.

It may stomp around in your world, making noise in your ears, causing you to be doubtful, distracted and continually rehashing your decisions with feelings of regret, inadequacy, or angst – and add to it the noise from social media shamers that bully and harass people with their harsh judgements.

This monster has an insidious way of making you second-guess your decisions and unfortunately negative behavioral patterns take root. As a person who crochets, I often notice patterns in things. So, to me I realized that negative behavioral patterns become very much like a flawed template that is reused, or repurposed, and more flawed garments are produced from it. Whether your past choices were mistakes or missteps that cannot be undone, or they were intentional choices based on your needs, morals, and priorities, or were hasty reactive choices made out of pressure, this monster wants you to forever rehash, relive and rethink what was done but not for the purpose of personal betterment, but to create self-limiting barriers and blessing-blocking veils.

Let's be clear; Feeling guilty for causing harm or pain to someone is right, decent, and is humane so I'm certainly not encouraging you to be callous, reckless, or insensitive as you are building your own happy life. What I do challenge you to do is identify the reasons for your guilt, the reasons this monster has such a tight grip onto you while soiling the good things currently in your life or sabotaging the rewarding things that you are trying to accomplish. Some of these things might include stronger friendships, spiritual awakening, a loving mate, a profitable business venture, or on the other hand is the reason you tolerate unhealthy relationships, have numerous unfinished goals, and find it difficult to make any forward momentum because of being stuck in the past.

The monster guilt is a bully that convinced you that cutting ties meant that you are an emotional brat, too independent, being selfish, or you will lose more than you would gain. This monster also wants you to stew in constant second-guessing, embarrassment, shame, or regret for decisions you've made. As long as you are in this guilt mode, you are closed to opportunities to heal, thrive, and learn, and cut off from receiving or giving anything good – as if you were someone undeserving or unworthy.

GET READY TO SLAY

FIGURATIVELY AND LITERALLY, THIS MONSTER GUILT pulls you downward. What does that downward disposition look and feel like? You may hang your head down in shame, hide from people, feel uneasy when certain topics come up, give lengthy justifications for your viewpoints, and likely missing out on occasions to see the beautiful, amazing, and even intoxicating things that could stimulate your senses, boost your interest in growth, and ignite your creativity. This monster holds you down by hoarding your gifts, blocking your joy, and crowding room in your heart and mind for openness, acceptance, and forgiveness. This state of living leads to defensiveness, anxiety, and self-consciousness because you're continually doubting your significance and ability to contribute or worthiness of happiness.

Self-confidence is the direct antithesis to prolonged, nagging guilt and its damaging effects. Self-confidence; however, is more than a momentary feeling of vanity, jubilance, or pride. It comes from the recognition of the things that are great about you, flaws, and all, and an ever awareness of continuous improvement out of gentle, regular self-love habits. These habits aren't solely based on fleeting material things but could include things like getting counselling, journaling, charitable community service activities, and creative outlets to express yourself in healthy ways – and potentially helping others too. There is a saying, 'If your circle isn't inspiring you to be a better person then it isn't a circle, but it is a cage'. Your circles of associates or friends shouldn't be a cage you're confined to that consists of judgmental hostiles, nor people that are mostly lip service enablers but are composed of growth-minded people.

Another byproduct is the feeling that you are a slave to an eternal debt that is imposed upon you as penance – real or imagined. Signs of this include reverse guilt where you past mistakes are held over you as a type of emotional blackmail, or if you are making strides toward betterment then you could be made to feel guilty due to your success and new lease on life.

Whether or not you think you actually "deserve" the guilt you harbor inside you, it's never a healthy emotion to hold onto in your life. This monster usually makes its painful and heavy appearance when you refuse to accept the fact that everyone makes mistakes, and we all have to deal with certain failures. (We discussed perfectionism in the previous chapter).

I realized that guilt can be a great motivation to correct something in your life that needs correcting, and once you've found a resolution, you'll begin to feel more at peace. Of course, in some cases, there will be unresolved guilt lurking around. This is when the emotion can be all-consuming, and you'll need to seek out ways to find inner peace.

When you want to free yourself from guilt, you first need to identify the reason why you feel the way you do. Let's take a look at some of the most common causes of guilt:

- You feel forced to remain in a valueless relationship or keep up appearances.
- You're not accepted by others or think the thoughts you're having are wrong.
- You feel responsible for something bad that has happened to you or someone else.
- You feel obligated to do something for someone for the wrong reasons.
- You never did something or said something important to someone and now you'll never get the chance.

When you've identified the reasons why you feel guilty, it's time to come to terms with the situation. If you continue spinning in a cycle of guilt, it won't be helping anyone, especially not you.

Leave the past in the past. If you've done something wrong (or something right but perhaps done in the wrong way), you must come to the realization that you can't change the past. Do what you can to make amends, learn from the situation, and then move on. The relationships may not be the same, but perhaps time and space is needed until then. That's all you can do.

If, however, you can fix the problem that's making you feel guilty, by all means, fix it as soon as possible. Beyond this, feeling guilty does not serve any purpose. Do what you can to overcome the situation and then release your guilty conscience.

Try not to be so hard on yourself. I had to wrestle with this tendency because I was frequently self-critical and adopted unrealistic expectations of myself. This may be easier said than done but you need to adjust your expectations to make them more realistic. If you've really given the situation your best shot and there's nothing else you can do, give yourself a break – your health and happiness is on the line.

Talking to select people can sometimes help. Perhaps a mature and trusted friend has been through a similar situation. If so, ask them about how they handled the situation and how you can make things better. For me, I included a therapist in my circle of trust for regular frank and honest discussions and goal setting.

Forgiving yourself is also key and this is something this monster does not expect you to do. It's in our human nature to make mistakes. Make a conscious effort to forgive yourself and your guilt will be released.

I want to take a moment to include a reality that sometimes impedes forgiveness of self – others who want you to remain eternally tormented. Sadly, there are many people who may try to bring you down and make you feel unnecessarily guilty. Some of these people may even be close to you. Make the conscious decision to disallow this kind of behavior. Strive for the confidence and awareness to prevent others from forcing guilty feelings onto you. This is a choice you can and should make for yourself. Feeling guilty all the time is unhealthy, both physically and mentally.

Once you properly release these harmful emotions, you'll feel like a tremendous weight has been lifted from your heart, mind, and shoulders and you'll be on your way to rebuilding your self-confidence and also self-acceptance. How?

Accepting yourself is the first step to building self-esteem and freeing yourself the painful grips of the monster guilt. It's not possible to feel positive about yourself if you can't even accept yourself. Self-acceptance is the level of happiness and satisfaction you have with yourself.

Accepting your flaws allows you the openness and willingness to change them. Learn to accept yourself and enjoy the person you are by considering some contributing factors:

Let go of your parents' behavior. If you've been conditioned from a young age to berate or nitpick at yourself, take steps now to unlearn these unhealthy traits. Seek out counselling to address the areas of your life that reflect beliefs or practices that no longer identify with the happy human being you are striving to becoming. Forgive them – forgive yourself - and release yourself from the past. Avoid judging yourself based on the parenting you received. It's a reflection of them, not you.

Find ways to give back to those in need, as your circumstances allow. Volunteering is an amazingly gratifying way to convince yourself that you're worthy of self-acceptance, and also being overly consumed in replaying your past in your mind. Prove to yourself how great a person you are. There are countless opportunities to volunteer in your community.

Be proud of your strengths. It's hard to accept yourself if you're constantly reminding yourself of your weaknesses. Make a long list that you can return to in the future. List every positive thing you can about yourself. Even the smallest positive attribute is worthy of mention.

Remember that everyone does the best they can. There will always be moments where you may not be the biggest or loudest star in the room, but it doesn't mean you aren't capable of shining your light or are less than deserving than anyone. Hold your head up high, learn from others, celebrate others, keep envy or competition at bay and remember your own gifts and talents – you Story.

Set realistic goals but accept changing timelines. It's difficult to accept yourself when the life you're living is quite different from your original plans. There's a time to tenaciously stay the course and checking off items on your to-do list but there's also a time to move a goal from the 1-year plan to the 5-year plan because of seen or unforeseen circumstances dictate the need to do so. Let the present moment be that time. Make new plans that are plausible and that excite you.

Eliminate negative self-talk. You can't accept yourself if you're constantly insulting yourself. Give yourself a fighting chance to reach a state of self-acceptance. Speak to yourself the way you would a good friend. Be a friend to yourself.

Be your authentic self. When you put on a persona for the world, you're not giving others the opportunity to accept you as you are. How will you be able to accept yourself and move beyond your guilt? When you're authentic, the love you feel for yourself and the love you receive feels infinitely more meaningful. Living honestly is scary, but surprisingly easy. People personally admire and professionally respect those with the strength to be authentic.

Recognize your worth and individual contributions to the world. Fortunately, this isn't something that must be earned like some penance. You're born with it. How much could you contribute if you applied yourself? The world needs you and all the good that you have to offer.

Forgive others. The ability to forgive others is intrinsically proportional to your ability to forgive yourself. I realized this is an absolutely non-negotiable thing. Practice forgiving others and you'll find self-acceptance comes much easier.

Self-acceptance is self-love and is the foundation for building up, forward and past latent guilt – it begins with giving credit, respect, honor, patience, and gentleness to yourself. No one is perfect. You accept your friends and family even though they're all flawed in a unique way. Give yourself the same latitude! Focus on your positive traits and forgive yourself for your flaws and mistakes. Accept yourself as you are – a beautiful work in progress!

I came to realize, in time, that I had to keep this monster from pulling my head and life down in perpetual shame and rehashing my missteps but to instead learn to leverage my successes and failures to my advantage. By doing this you recognize what works and what doesn't work, and then apply that knowledge to the future. You become more capable, knowledgeable, and powerful with each passing day. You evolve into a successful and capable person.

However, most people fail to use their experiences to their advantage. They avoid failure and examining those times they do fail. Success is seen as a time for celebrating, not learning. But this is a great mistake! The rules of life are revealed to you each day.

I want you to use your imagination. Imagine if you used every experience to become an enhanced version of yourself. Imagine if you learned from every mistake and every success. What if you repeated jut a fewer number of mistakes and made the most of your successes? How would your life change in a year? In 10 years? The results could be amazing!

I have the following process that can help you make your successes and failures work for you.

Examine your past. Think back on your life and make a list of all your greatest successes and failures. Think about your work, educational, and relationship experiences. Think about those times you made plans and came up short or experienced considerable success. Consider why you were successful. What made you successful? Consider why you failed. What can you learn from that that you can apply to the future?

Determine your purpose for each day. Successes and failures are often the result of little successes and failures each day. Setting a standard for the day provides a benchmark for determining your success that day. I have found this kept another related monster from getting in my way – reactive living versus proactive living.

Review and pursue your long-term goals. You need long-term goals to measure your successes and failures against. Long-term goals also allow you to plan your day more effectively rather than being solely propelled by emotions or impulsivity.

Take time to review your day. At the end of your day, review how well you stuck to your plan. Develop a routine for yourself – during your drive home, bath time, prayer, or meditation time, or even while organizing your wardrobe and supplies for the next day. What did you succeed at today? What did you fail at? What were the factors that led to those successes and failures?

Determine ways to improve. After reviewing your day, what changes do you want to make for tomorrow? How can you be better tomorrow than you were today? What can you do tomorrow that will make you 1% better than you were today? Make a new plan for tomorrow that includes the lessons that you identified today.

Go ahead and test your ideas and hypotheses – this will keep you creative rather than rigid. Spend a day executing your new plan. Did you have a better day? What were your failures today? What were your successes? What can you do to have an even better day tomorrow?

I love journaling. Try it. A journal can be a great tool for making the most of your successes and failures. You'll learn things from your past and your present that can be applied to your future. Each day provides you with information that can be used to enhance your approach to life. Leverage your successes and failures to become the most successful version of yourself.

Everything seems easier when you're brimming with self-confidence. Self-confidence provides a solid foundation for living a life of happiness and accomplishing great things. Unfortunately, it seems like the world is doing everything in its power to destroy whatever self-confidence you might enjoy.

Your opinion of yourself shapes your beliefs, behaviors, and outcomes. As you're rebuilding your self-confidence, start small and include taking care of your health (diet, exercise, boundaries), home (I especially feel good after purging junk that I held onto for the wrong reasons), deleting unnecessary contact, cleaning your social media feed, review an upcoming goal such as savings, or vacation, or special work project.

I've said this before, but I really believe it can't be overstated - Take control of your internal dialog. Notice the negative things you say to yourself and quickly edit them into a more positive version. This requires time and energy, but the payoff is huge.

Being prepared reduces stress and boosts confidence to make the decisions you need to make. Whether you have a presentation at work, a meeting with your attorney, a date, or an overdue conversation with a friend, be prepared. Wear clothes that fit the occasion. Who will be there? What do you need to know? How can you best prepare? What are possible outcomes? What is my objective? What are my non-negotiables? You'll feel much more confident when you're highly prepared.

Enjoy the success. Rather than feeding thoughts that you aren't deserving, you dismiss compliments, or diminishing its significance, savor each victory. You'll have the confidence to gradually go after a bigger one. A steady stream of victories is the surest way to boost your self-confidence. You'll feel like there's nothing you can't do.

Iron sharpens iron. Surround yourself with those that support your happiness. Spend time with others who encourage you. You only need a few good friends to make life worthwhile – here is where quality rather than quantity matters. Consider trimming your social circle and keep the people that routinely treat you the best.

Here's something I still do, and I keep on my vision board: Make a list of your strengths, talents, and accomplishments. Rather than focusing on the things you don't do well, or failed at, spend some time being positive. What are your greatest achievements? What do you do well? What are your strengths? Make a long list and keep writing until you've run out of ideas. You'll be warmed by how amazing you are. Focus on your personal progress and forget about making comparisons to others.

Self-confidence is arsenal that this monster doesn't expect you to regularly fortify so it is fueled by your thoughts, the company you keep, and your acts that aren't based on your personal truths and values. So never neglect this essential part of your personal growth plan – your happiness depends on it. Self-confidence gives you the power to change your life and slay that ugly guilt monster once and for all!

AFFIRMATIONS

I am worthy of my goals.

I am allowed to have lofty goals. I am worthy of goals that are ambitious. My heart and soul are set on achieving them. My body and spirit are determined to make them real. I know I can do whatever is required to bring my dreams to life.

My efforts are paying off. I have clear targets to reach.

My goals of having abundance, love, and happiness are worthwhile.

My career ambitions are also worth pursuing and within my reach.

I am allowed to have big dreams.

I am worthy of getting what I want. I deserve to have health, love, and money. I have the right to enjoy my life.

My dreams are worth pursuing. I know that I deserve to have success.

I have support and encouragement to help me reach my goals. My coworkers, family, and friends help me along the way. They uplift me when I doubt myself and celebrate with me when I hit milestones toward my goals.

I learn from my mistakes and pay attention to details. As a result, I avoid many challenges and reach my goals easier.

Today, I notice my own value and how my goals support me. I know they are within reach. I feel ready to make my dreams a reality.

SELF-REFLECTION QUESTIONS:

4. Do I feel worthy of lofty goals? What can I do to strengthen my self-esteem and move past guilt?
5. Is it possible to reach my goals faster? How?
6. How do I know when it is time to set new goals or rewrite the current ones?

EPILOGUE

IF YOU'RE NOT ACTIVELY PURSUING YOUR DREAMS, a fear is likely to blame. Fear can stop you from taking the actions necessary for you to achieve genuine happiness and success.

Fear isn't something to be avoided. Use fear to your advantage. Fear is a wonderful opportunity to learn about yourself. Fear can also be used as chance to grow on a personal level. If you're not afraid, you're not living.

It is my hope that within these pages you've been able to relate to my battles with my own monsters over the years, and you made notes of strategies you can begin implementing right away. Courage is key! You'd be shocked by how much your life would change if you could just increase your courage by 10%! That's all it takes. Courage creates action, which boosts your courage even higher. Follow these strategies to increase your courage and accomplish more:

Visualize success. Fear comes from many sources, as we learned, but mostly from imagining the worst, so one solution is to imagine a positive outcome. It's important to make the visualization as real as possible. Use all of your senses to create a realistic scene. Imagine how you'll feel when you're successful. Let it be as if you can taste, smell, feel touch and hear it becoming a reality.

Do this regularly and it will make a difference. Employing this technique even one time can be enough to take the edge off your fear and allow you to act.

"A little progress each day adds up to big results."

— Anonymous

Imagine your child, mentee, or trusted friend is watching you. It's easy to take the easy way out when you're alone. Have you ever noticed that the presence of an audience makes you a little bolder? No one wants to lose face in front of their peers especially when you are in a position to motivate, teach and inspire others. Tell yourself that you're going to set a good example.

Ask yourself what a brave person would do – your hero, a person that you admire and respect. To motivate yourself, think of someone you know that's brave and contemplate how they would handle the situation you're in.

Remember how short life is and the regret you'll feel if you failed to act. Instead of thinking about failure, think about the consequences of never trying. Regret is a painful pill to swallow. Give yourself the chance to be successful. The last thing anyone wants is to spend the latter part of life wondering "what if?"

Change your physiology. Breathe deeply. You're your head up, look straight ahead, stand the way a king or queen would stand. Imagine yourself as an even more successful, knowledgeable, and confident person. Remember how that monster wants to pull down your countenance, your disposition, your confidence, and your presence. It just takes a small boost in courage to get the ball rolling.

I've tackled and slayed many monsters in my life. Some of them left very faint scars and others left some pretty prominent ones. Once I made up my mind to face them rather than ignore them, recognize how they were being fueled and identifying the symptoms of their impact on my happiness, I got serious, got my battle plan together, got focused, and got determined to put up a strong fight for my happiness, success, and peace – I knew that's what I deserved and could have. I know this for you too.

You too can be a slayer of monsters. You can conquer your fears and be even more amazing that you already are! Roar louder, fight harder, dig deeper, stretch farther, take the offensive position of attack, and show no mercy. Remember to always arm yourself everyday with the knowledge you've gained, knowing your monster is always waiting for an opening to sabotage your happiness. Remember what fuels your fears because when you know the weaknesses of those monsters, you have the advantage over them.

You are ready!

Now, go Slay!

ABOUT THE AUTHOR

Da-Nel has been a lifelong writer and in 2011 she released her first book, "Broke and Alone – A Woman's Guide for Introspective Living". Her writing style has been described as 'vivid, honest, funny, metaphorical, and inspiring'. As a Certified Professional Development Trainer and National Motivational Speaker, she has successfully demonstrated her passion for challenging individuals across the country to live a life of fulfillment, growth, honesty, and joy.

Da-Nel has created the curriculum for several education programs tailored to women-owned small businesses, and she has received numerous recognition awards including an honorable Citation for her humanitarian efforts.

When she is not teaching, travelling or writing Da-Nel finds joy on hiking trails, gardening, discovering new Scotch Whiskeys, passionately cheering for her favorite sports teams, baking for her family, and fussing over her plump tuxedo cat.

Made in the USA
Las Vegas, NV
17 April 2021